NED KELLY
A True Story

Australia in the 1870s was a new country for Europeans. They came from England and Ireland and Scotland to begin a new life. Some families had good land for farming and got rich. But others were poor, and stayed poor. It was a hard life, and a hard life makes hard young men – like the wild Kelly boys.

Policemen in those early years in Australia were hard men too. Some of them were not very interested in justice. They just wanted to win the fight. There were a lot of fights with the Kelly boys – and not much justice. That is the way to drive wild young men outside the law.

Ned Kelly stole horses, was often in trouble, and did not like policemen. They put his mother, Ellen Kelly, in prison for three years. Ellen and Ned tried to kill a policeman, they said. But it was not true. What can a man do when that happens? He becomes an outlaw – and fights back . . .

OXFORD BOOKWORMS LIBRARY
True Stories

Ned Kelly
A True Story
Stage 1 (400 headwords)

Series Editor: Jennifer Bassett
Founder Editor: Tricia Hedge
Activities Editors: Jennifer Bassett and Christine Lindop

CHRISTINE LINDOP

Ned Kelly

A True Story

OXFORD UNIVERSITY PRESS

OXFORD

UNIVERSITY PRESS

Great Clarendon Street, Oxford OX2 6DP

Oxford University Press is a department of the University of Oxford.
It furthers the University's objective of excellence in research, scholarship,
and education by publishing worldwide in

Oxford New York

Auckland Cape Town Dar es Salaam Hong Kong Karachi Kuala Lumpur
Madrid Melbourne Mexico City Nairobi New Delhi Shanghai Taipei Toronto

With offices in

Argentina Austria Brazil Chile Czech Republic France Greece
Guatemala Hungary Italy Japan Poland Portugal Singapore
South Korea Switzerland Thailand Turkey Ukraine Vietnam

OXFORD and OXFORD ENGLISH are registered trade marks of
Oxford University Press in the UK and in certain other countries

ISBN 978 0 19 478912 7

A complete recording of this Bookworms edition of
Ned Kelly is available on audio CD ISBN 978 0 19 478847 2

Printed in Hong Kong

ACKNOWLEDGEMENTS

Original illustrations by: David Eaton pp 2, 5, 9, 13, 18, 23, 33, 35, 39, 50

*The publishers would like to thank the following for their permission to reproduce photographs and other
copyright material:* Australian Manuscripts Collection, State Library of Victoria p 26; Noel O'Shea
p 32; Private Collection pp 1, 20, 28 (Joe Byrne, Steve Hart), 30; © State of Victoria. Reproduced
with the permission of the Keeper of Public Records, Public Record Office Victoria,
Australia/PROV, VPRS8369/P1, Unit 1, Photograph of Edward Kelly p 6; La Trobe Picture
Collection, State Library of Victoria pp 28 (Dan Kelly, Steve Hart), 30, 37, 40, 42; Victoria Police
Historical Unit Melbourne Australia pp 11, 16, 28 (Ned Kelly); Westpac Historical Services p 24.

Special thanks to Matt Shore and Ian Jones for their great help in supplying pictures.

The cover photograph is from the motion picture *Ned Kelly* (2003) featuring Heath Ledger, and licensed
courtesy of Universal Studios LLLP. The publishers have made every effort to contact any other copyright
holders, but have been unable to do so. If copyright holders would like to contact them, the publishers
would be happy to pay an appropriate reproduction fee.

Word count (main text): 5774 words

For more information on the Oxford Bookworms Library,
visit www.oup.com/bookworms

CONTENTS

Ned Kelly in prison, the day before he died

IT IS THE YEAR 1880.

In the prison in Melbourne, Australia, a young man has visitors – his mother, a brother, and two sisters. Nobody is saying very much. There is only one word to say, and the word is 'Goodbye'.

Because the young man is Ned Kelly, the most famous outlaw in all Australia. And tomorrow morning the prison officers are going to put a rope around his neck and hang him until he is dead.

Ned Kelly

This is Ned Kelly's story . . .

1

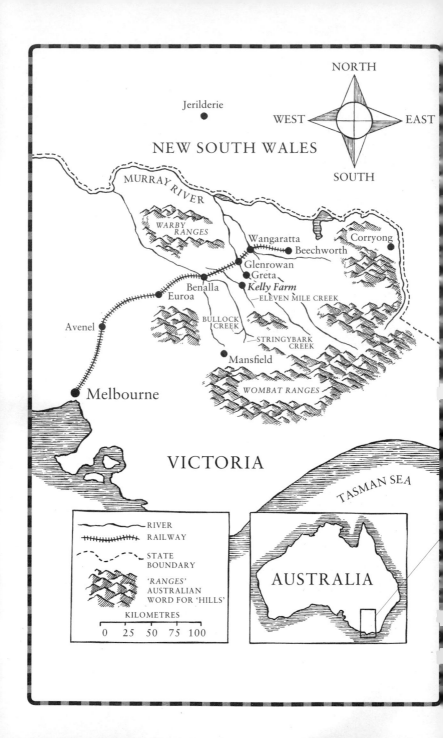

1

Ned's young days

JULY, 1865. The story begins in Avenel, a small town north of Melbourne. Ned Kelly lives here with his parents, John and Ellen Kelly. Ned is ten years old, the oldest boy of the seven Kelly children. He has two brothers, Jim and Dan, and four sisters – Anne, Maggie, Kate, and Grace.

✗ ✗ ✗

'Where's your father, boy?' Ellen Kelly called out to her son one evening. 'Is he on the road? Can you see him?'

Ned Kelly looked out of the door. 'No, Ma,' he said. 'I can't see him.'

Ned's father came home late, and he came in quietly.

'Ellen,' he said, 'come with me. I need your help. There's a dead cow by the trees on the hill. We must cut it up and bring it home.'

'Oh, John, is it one of our cows?' his wife asked. 'How did it die?'

'It's one of Morgan's cows, and I killed it,' John said. 'So we must be quick, before he comes looking for it.'

'Oh, you fool!' said Ellen.

In the children's bed in the next room, Ned listened to this. It was a small house, with only two rooms, and you could hear everything. Ned was pleased about the dead

3

cow. They didn't often have meat to eat, and the children were always hungry.

But dead cows bring trouble. Three days later there was a policeman at the door. 'John Kelly, you killed Morgan's cow, and I'm taking you to prison . . .'

That was the end of school for Ned Kelly. He was the man of the family now. He helped his mother, and he worked on the Kellys' farm. The farm was not very big, and life was not easy for the Kellys.

John Kelly and Ellen Quinn were from Ireland. They first met in Melbourne, and then came north, to find land for a farm. Many other Irish people did the same thing. Everybody wanted land, but some people had a lot more land than other people. It was a hard, wild life. There was a lot of drinking, a lot of fighting, a lot of stealing – horses, cows, dead or alive . . .

John Kelly was in prison for six months. Prison was not good for him, and when he came out, he began to drink. A year and a half later he was dead.

'What are we going to do now, Ma?' Ned asked.

Ellen thought about it. She was a tall, strong woman, and all her life she was a fighter. She had twelve children in the end and was ninety-three years old when she died.

'We must leave here,' she said. 'We must go to the north-east, and live near my family.'

x x x

The Kellys' new house was at Eleven Mile Creek, near Greta. They had some animals and a small garden, and Ned worked hard to get money for the family. He could do farming work, take care of horses and cows, cut down trees.

It was a hard, wild life.

Ned Kelly, 15 years old

But trouble was never far away. The police did not like the wild Kelly boys, or their friends. In 1870, when Ned was fifteen, he hit a man very hard in a fight, and the police put him in prison for six months.

The next year something worse happened. Ned was in the town of Greta on a brown horse when Policeman Hall came up to him.

'Ned Kelly, you get down and come with me. You stole that horse and I'm taking you to prison.'

'That's not true,' said Ned, and then there was a terrible fight. Policeman Hall had a gun and Ned did not, but Ned was the better fighter. In the end Hall called for help and five men came to help him.

Next day they took Ned down to Wangaratta and he went in front of the judge.

'It's not my horse, it belongs to a man called Wild Wright,' Ned told the judge. 'Wright was at my mother's house, and his horse ran away. He needed a horse so I gave him one of my horses. And he said to me, "When you find the brown horse, you keep her for me." And so when I found the horse, I kept her.'

'Ned Kelly stole that horse!' Policeman Hall said. 'It belongs to a man in Mansfield, and someone stole it on the 6th of March.'

'Well,' Ned said, 'I was in Beechworth prison up to the 29th of March. How can I steal a horse when I'm in prison? And Wright told me it was *his* horse – I didn't know it was a stolen horse.'

But it is a crime to have a stolen horse. Wild Wright, of course, stole the horse, and he went to prison for eighteen months. But they put Ned Kelly in prison for three years. When he came back to Eleven Mile Creek in 1874, things were very different.

2
The Kelly Gang

MAY, 1874. Ned's sister Annie is dead; his brother Jim is in prison (five years for stealing cows), and his brother Dan is often in trouble too. There are new faces at home – a new husband, and a new baby, for Ned's mother.

x x x

'Ned? Is that you? Oh, Ned!' Ellen Kelly ran to the door. Ned, now nineteen years old, tall and strong, was home from prison. He put his arm round his mother.

'Hello, Ma,' he said.

'Oh, Ned, it's good to see you,' said Ellen.

'I heard about Jim,' Ned said. 'And little Annie.'

'Poor, poor Annie,' said his mother. 'She was so ill after she had the baby, and we couldn't do anything to help her. And poor Jim got five years!'

'Yes, that's hard,' said Ned. 'And what about you, Ma? I hear you've got a new husband.' He looked at the sleeping baby in his mother's arms.

'He's a good man, Ned. Little Ellen here – she's his daughter.'

Ned touched the baby's little hand.

'I'm happy for you, Ma. And I'm happy to be back.'

x x x

Ned soon found work. He moved from farm to farm, cutting down trees and helping with the horses and cows. He often came home to see his mother, and he and George King, Ellen's new husband, were soon friends. George was from California, and was only five years older than Ned.

Ned soon found work, cutting down trees.

On one visit home, Ned talked to George about the police. 'Why do they give me all this trouble?' he said.

'I don't know,' said George. 'They just don't like you.'

'It's true,' Ned said. 'When somebody loses a cow or a horse, the police always come to *me* with their questions. Then they go to my mother's house and ask *her* questions. And they always go late at night, when you're all in bed. It isn't right.'

'Well, come and work with me,' said George. 'Why not? *You're* good with horses, and *I* don't have any trouble with the police.'

'What work are you planning to do?' said Ned.

'Sell horses – lots of them.'

'And where are you going to get all these horses from, George?' asked Ned.

George smiled. And Ned laughed.

x x x

It was exciting work. 'We stole 280 horses,' Ned said later. 'Then we took them across the Murray River and sold them in New South Wales for a lot of money.'

The police got angrier and angrier. They couldn't stop the stealing, and they couldn't catch Ned Kelly or George King with the stolen horses.

In August 1877 a new policeman came to Benalla. Alex Fitzpatrick liked horses, girls, and drink, and for some weeks he and Ned were friends. Ned's sister Kate was a

Policeman Alex Fitzpatrick, in 1877

beautiful girl with long black hair. She liked Fitzpatrick too, at first. But soon there were angry words between him and Ned, and then a fight. A policeman could not be a friend of the Kellys for long.

April 1878 came. The police had questions about stolen horses for Dan, and for Ned's best friend, Joe Byrne. So Fitzpatrick rode out to the Kellys' house, to find Dan. Perhaps he wanted to see Kate too – but did Kate want to see him? On his way there he stopped and had two or three drinks. When he arrived at the house, he felt very strong and brave.

'Dan Kelly, you're coming with me to the police station,' he said.

'I'm having my dinner,' said Dan. 'You can wait.'

Fitzpatrick sat at the table, waiting for Dan, but his eyes were on Kate all the time – on her long black hair, on her beautiful body. The small room felt very hot.

Then Kate walked past the table, very near him, and he put his arm around her.

'You're a beautiful girl, Kate,' he said. 'Let's—'

'Take your hands off me!' said Kate.

Suddenly Ned was at the door, with a gun in his hand. He fired at Fitzpatrick and hit him in the wrist.

'Get out!' said Ned. 'Get away from my sister!'

Fitzpatrick ran out of the house and rode through the night back to Benalla.

The next morning there were ten policemen at the door. They found Ellen at home, but not Ned or Dan.

'Ellen Kelly,' they said. 'You and your sons tried to kill Policeman Fitzpatrick.'

'Nobody tried to kill Fitzpatrick!' said Ellen. 'You just want to make trouble for me and my family.' She had a new baby in her arms, her third child by George King. But George did not live with Ellen now.

'Mrs Kelly, where are your sons?' said a policeman.

Ellen looked into the policeman's eyes. 'I don't know,' she said. 'You want them, you go and find them.'

x x x

'Get out!' said Ned. 'Get away from my sister!'

13

When Ned and Dan left their mother's house that night, they rode away into the Wombat Hills. At Bullock Creek, miles from anywhere, they built a small hut. They lived wild, and looked for gold in the river.

Joe Byrne, Ned's good friend, went with them, because he needed to hide from the police too. And in June, three months later, Steve Hart, another good friend, came out of prison. He, too, got on his horse and rode to Bullock Creek. So there were four of them.

Then, in October, Ellen's brother came to find them, with some terrible news.

'Your mother's going to prison, Ned. For three years. Because she and you and Dan tried to kill Fitzpatrick, the judge said. And the police are looking for you and Dan. Be careful, boys – stay in the hills!'

For a second Ned's eyes were red like fire. He spoke slowly and coldly.

'They can look,' he said, 'but they can't catch me out here.' He looked at his brother Dan and his friends Joe and Steve. 'These policemen, these judges – they're worse than dogs! They put my mother in prison, and what did she do? Nothing! From now on, we're the Kelly gang. We're free men – and we're staying that way. Are you with me, boys?'

And that was the beginning of the Kelly Gang.

3
Three dead men

OCTOBER, 1878. Four policemen ride north from the town of Mansfield. Kennedy, McIntyre, Lonigan, and Scanlon are on their way to Stringybark Creek in the Wombat Hills. They plan to camp there for a week, look for the Kelly Gang – and bring them back to Mansfield, dead or alive.

x x x

Very early one morning Ned and Dan left Bullock Creek. Joe and Steve waited at the hut.

'Walk quietly, Dan,' said Ned, 'and listen. I saw horses' tracks near here yesterday, and I think the police are after us.'

The police camp at Stringybark Creek was only two kilometres away, and the brothers soon found it. They hid behind the trees and watched. They saw the four policemen, and their guns – two big heavy guns and four smaller guns.

Later, back at Bullock Creek, Joe and Steve listened to the news about the guns.

'We've only got two guns. What can we do?' said Joe.

'They want to kill us,' said Dan. 'They're going to shoot to kill. Isn't that right, Ned?'

'Yes, that's right,' said Ned. 'So, we can stay here and

Policeman Thomas McIntyre

wait for them – or we can go down there and take their guns and horses. What do you say?'

It was an easy answer. The Kelly Gang got ready, left Bullock Creek, and went quietly through the trees.

When they arrived at the police camp, only Lonigan and McIntyre were there. Lonigan sat on a tree, reading a newspaper, and McIntyre watched the camp fire. Then, from behind a tree, Ned Kelly called out.

'Put your hands up!'

McIntyre had no gun, so he sat still and put his hands up,

but Lonigan ran. Then he got down behind a fallen tree, took out his gun, and put his head up.

He was a fool. A bullet from Ned's gun hit him in the head, and he died at once.

Ned ran to McIntyre. 'Don't move!' he said. 'We don't want to kill you, we just want the guns and horses.'

But before the gang could find the guns and leave, they heard a noise in the trees.

'Ned!' called Steve. 'The other two policemen are coming back!'

'Sit on this tree,' Ned said to McIntyre. 'And when you see your friends, call out to them. Say, "Don't shoot – put your guns on the ground." We don't want to kill them, or you.'

Seconds later, Kennedy and Scanlon rode into the camp. McIntyre stood up and said, 'Get off your horses and put your hands up – there are men with guns here.'

'Oh yes?' said Kennedy. He laughed at McIntyre. 'What men? What guns?'

At once the Kelly Gang came out of the trees and Ned called, 'Put your hands up!'

Everything happened very quickly. A bullet from Ned's gun hit Scanlon, and he fell from his horse. Kennedy jumped off his horse and fired at Dan. Dan fired back, and Kennedy ran back into the trees.

McIntyre could not shoot because he did not have his

The gunfight at Stringybark Creek

gun with him. But there in front of him was Kennedy's horse. He jumped on it and rode into the trees.

Kennedy tried to get away too. He went quietly through the trees, but suddenly he saw Ned in front of him. The two men fired – and Kennedy fell down. Soon he was dead.

'He was a brave man, but it was him or me,' said Ned. 'I didn't want to do it. I didn't want to kill any of them.'

The gang put coats over the three dead bodies, took the horses, guns and food, and rode away.

'They came to kill us, boys,' said Ned, 'but we killed them. What could we do? Now we must go – and we're not coming back.'

The Kelly Gang rode away to the north.

x x x

The next day, tired and dirty, McIntyre arrived back in Mansfield. Soon every town and village and farm in the north-east knew about the killing of the three policemen at Stringybark Creek.

'The Kelly Gang are killers,' said the police. 'These men are now outlaws, and we must catch them, dead or alive. When you see them, tell us. We are giving £500 reward for news of every man in the gang £2000 for all four of them.'

It was a lot of money. More policemen came to the north-east, with more guns, more horses.

Ned and the gang stayed in the north-east. They tried to

The reward for news of the Kelly Gang

get away to the north, but there was a lot of water in the Murray River, and they couldn't get across it. They got help from their friends and moved from place to place all the time. One week they rode more than three hundred kilometres.

Thirty policemen rode through the hills for a month and looked for the outlaws night and day. But they never found them, and in December Ned and the gang moved on to the Warby Hills. It was a hard, wild life, and the outlaws were tired, hungry, and angry men.

4

Two visits to the bank

DECEMBER, 1878. The Kelly Gang have many friends, but they have no money. So they rob the bank in the little town of Euroa. They speak nicely to the people in the town, and do not fire their guns. They leave Euroa with £2260. But they give a lot of the money to their friends, the poor farmers of the north-east, to buy food, clothes, and land. The police reward goes up to £2500.

x x x

The police tried hard to catch the Kelly Gang, but the outlaws had help from their friends. They were always miles away when the police came to look for them. So the police put many of their friends in prison.

Ned was very angry about this. 'It isn't right!' he said. 'Why do the police do this? Because our friends are poor farmers, not rich ones, and because they help us. We must stop the police!'

'But how?' said Steve. 'What can we do?'

'Two things,' said Ned. 'First, we need more money, so we must visit a bank. And second, we tell everybody in Australia about the police here in Victoria.'

'Rob another bank?' Dan said. 'But the police are watching all the banks now.'

21

'Yes, in Victoria,' said Ned. 'But not in New South Wales, so we're going to a bank in Jerilderie. Here's the plan. There are only two policemen in Jerilderie. We arrive at night, go to the police station, and lock the policemen in the station. Then we rob the bank, and go to the office of Jerilderie's newspaper.'

'The newspaper office?' said Dan. 'Why? What for?'

'To print this,' said Joe. 'Look. It's Ned's letter to the world. I wrote it down for him. It tells the true story about Ned and his family, about the police, about Stringybark Creek, about everything.'

'We want everybody to read this letter, but how do we give it to them?' Ned said. 'We must print it in a newspaper. It's the only way.'

x x x

Ned planned the Jerilderie visit very carefully. There were now more than two hundred policemen in the north-east of Victoria because of the Kelly Gang, and Ned asked his friend Aaron Sherritt for help.

So Aaron went drinking with a policeman. Money passed from one hand to another, and Aaron spoke quietly in the policeman's ear.

'Go to Corryong. The gang are planning to cross the Murray River near there very soon.'

So the police rode east to Corryong – and the Kelly Gang rode west, and crossed the river two hundred kilometres away. And late on a Saturday night in February 1879, they rode into the town of Jerilderie.

Outside the police station Ned began to shout, 'Help! Help! There's a big fight at the hotel! We need help!'

The two policemen ran out – and saw the outlaws with their guns. The gang locked the policemen in a room in the station, and took their uniforms.

*The two policemen ran out – and saw
the outlaws with their guns.*

The bank at Jerilderie.
The man in the doorway is Edwin Living.

For the next two days the gang lived in the police station. On Sunday Joe and Steve put on the police uniforms and walked around the town. 'We're the new policemen for Jerilderie,' they told everyone. They went past the bank and the hotel next to it, and looked carefully at all the doors, front and back.

Then, on Monday morning Dan and Steve went into the hotel next to the bank, and took out their guns. They took all the hotel workers into one room.

'Don't move,' said Dan. 'You're our hostages, but don't be afraid. We don't want to shoot anybody.'

Ned and Joe went into the bank through the back door. When they came back to the hotel, they had more hostages

– two bank workers and all the people from the bank. And Ned had the bank's money – £2140.

There were now about sixty hostages in the room, and Ned began to speak to them.

'What's happening in this country? Do you know? No, you don't! So listen! Poor men get poorer, and rich men get richer. The police help the rich farmers, and put the poor farmers in prison. Why? For nothing! Do you call this justice? There *is* no justice in Australia!

'The police say we are killers. But I say the police are killers! I'm going to tell you about Stringybark Creek – the true story, not the police story.'

Ned began to read to the hostages from his letter. It was a long letter, 56 pages and more than 75,000 words. After a few pages he stopped.

'Where's the newspaper office in this town?' he said. 'I want to print this letter. Then everybody can read it.'

Edwin Living, one of the bank workers, answered.

'Mr Gill is the editor of the newspaper,' he said. 'I know his house. I can take you there.'

'Come on, then,' Ned said.

But Mr Gill was not at home. He was at a farm ten kilometres away. When he heard the Kelly Gang were in town, he ran away, because he was afraid of them.

At the house Mrs Gill opened the door.

'Where's your husband?' Ned asked.

41

behind the tree my brother Dan advanced
and Kennedy ran I followed him he
stopped behind another tree and
fired again I shot him in the arm
pit and he dropped his revolver and
ran I fired again with the gun as
he slewed around to surrender I did
not know he had dropped his revolver
the bullet passed through the right
side of his chest & he could not live
or I would have let him go had they
been my own brothers I could not help
shooting them or else let them shoot me
which they would have done had their
bullets been directed as they intended
them. But as for handcuffing Kennedy
to a tree or cutting his ear off or bru
tally treating any of them is a false
hood, if Kennedys ear was cut off
it was not done by me and none

A page from the Jerilderie Letter

'I – I don't know. He's – he's away,' Mrs Gill said.

Ned looked at her angrily, and took out his letter. 'I want him to print this in his newspaper,' he said.

'Give it to me,' said Edwin Living. 'I can give it to Mr Gill when he gets back.'

'He must print it,' said Ned. 'It's about my life, and I want the world to read it.'

'Yes,' said Edwin. 'Everybody must read it. And Mr Gill's going to print it – for sure, Mr Kelly.'

'He must,' Ned said. 'All right, you give it to him. But do it! Or the next time I come to Jerilderie . . .'

They went back to the hotel, and Ned had a drink with the hostages. Then the four outlaws rode out of town, back to the Murray River, and across into Victoria and the hills in the north-east.

✳ ✳ ✳

The police looked everywhere. They made the reward £8,000, but nobody came to get it. Nobody wanted to help them. In Jerilderie, people laughed about the visit of the Kelly Gang. In April, Ned's friends came out of prison and went back to their farms. And for sixteen months, the police heard nothing of the Kelly Gang.

And Ned's letter – the famous 'Jerilderie Letter'?

Edwin Living did not give it to Mr Gill. He went down to Melbourne and gave it to the police.

Nobody saw the letter again for fifty years.

THE KELLY GANG

Ned Kelly

Dan Kelly

Joe Byrne

Steve Hart

5

Alive or dead at Glenrowan

JUNE, 1880. The Kelly Gang are living in the hills. Their friends bring them food, but life is hard, and the police are still making trouble. They don't put the Kellys' friends in prison now, but they stop them buying land. And why? Because they are friends of the Kelly Gang . . .

x x x

'We must do something,' Ned said, 'to help our friends. We need a new country – a country for poor people, with good police, and good judges. But it's not going to happen easily. We must fight for it!'

'We need money for that,' said Joe. 'A lot of money. And there's a policeman with a gun at every bank now.'

'We need armour, to go over our heads and bodies,' Ned said. 'Bullets can't get through armour.'

'How are we going to get armour?' asked Dan.

'We can make it,' said Ned.

And they did. With help from their friends, they made four suits of armour from old farm machinery. Then they began to plan their fight.

'Our friends want to help,' Ned said. 'They have guns, and they want to fight with us. So we need to bring a lot of policemen to one place. How can we do that?'

Ned Kelly's armour

'With a killing,' said Joe. 'We kill Aaron Sherritt. He's working for the police – he tells them everything about us! You know it, I know it, everybody knows it. He was a friend once, but now he wants to see us dead!'

'Yes, that's true,' Ned said. 'We hear it from everybody. So, you go to Aaron's house at Beechworth and shoot him. You and Dan.'

'Right,' said Dan. 'And then when the Beechworth police hear about the killing, they know it's us, the Kelly Gang. So they ask for help from the police at Benalla . . .'

'And the Benalla police take the train to Beechworth,' said Steve. 'Lots of police, all in one train.'

'And we', Ned said quietly, 'are waiting for the train at Glenrowan . . .'

30

The plan began well. Joe and Dan rode to Beechworth. When Aaron Sherritt opened his door on Saturday 26th June, Joe shot him at once. Then the two outlaws rode sixty kilometres across country to Glenrowan. News of the killing went down to Benalla.

Ned and Steve arrived at Glenrowan Inn on Saturday afternoon. They began to bring hostages into the inn – people from the railway station, railway workers, people from the town. Then Ned took some of the railway workers to the hill just past the railway station.

'Take up the railway line,' he told them. 'Go on!'

'We can't do that!' one worker said. 'Do you want to kill everybody on the next train?'

Then he saw Ned's gun, and asked no more questions. The workers took up three metres of railway line, and went back to the inn with Ned. Joe and Dan were there now, and some of the gang's friends. Other friends, about thirty men, stayed near the railway line. In the inn there was a lot of drinking that night.

On Sunday morning Ned found more hostages – the schoolteacher, Thomas Curnow, with his young wife, baby, and sister. There were now sixty-two hostages in the inn. And everybody waited for the police train.

The police moved very slowly. In Beechworth, Benalla, and Melbourne they talked, made plans, and talked some more. In the end, a police train left Melbourne late on Sunday evening. And that evening Ned told about twenty of the hostages, 'You can go home.' Later, the schoolteacher came to him.

'Can I take my family home?' he asked. 'Don't be afraid of me – you know I'm a friend of the Kellys.'

'Yes, you can go,' said Ned.

Thomas Curnow was a brave man. He took his young family home, and later went quietly out into the night and along the railway line. At three o'clock in the morning he heard the train, and held up a red light.

'Stop! Stop!' he cried.

Thomas Curnow, the Glenrowan schoolteacher

✗ ✗ ✗

At the inn, Ned and the gang heard the train too. They listened, but there was no noise of a crash, no train falling through the trees, no cries and shouts.

'What's happening?' Steve said.

'Nothing,' said Ned. 'Somebody stopped the train before it got to the broken rails. Put your armour on, boys, and get ready to fight.'

Curnow heard the train, and held up a red light.

The gang went out to the front of the inn. They began to fire at the police, and the police fired back. Bullets went everywhere.

33

Three of the hostages inside the inn died. The police shot Ned in the arm and the foot, and Joe in the leg.

'Go back into the inn,' Ned said to the gang. 'I must find our friends. They must get away from here.'

The gang's friends were near the railway line.

'We want to fight, Ned,' they said. 'Take us with you!'

'No, no, you must get away,' said Ned. 'The plan for the train went wrong, and there are police everywhere. This is our fight. You can't help us! Go!'

Back at the inn, the shooting did not stop. The hostages, many of them women and children, were on the floor, their faces white and afraid. Joe was in the front room with a drink in his hand.

'I drink to the Kelly Gang!' he cried. Then a bullet came through the wall and hit him. He died at once.

The wounds in Ned's arm and foot were bad, and in the trees he fell to the ground. A friend tried to help him, but for some hours Ned could not move. Then, slowly, he stood up, and in his armour began to walk back to the inn. His brother Dan and Steve Hart were still inside the inn, and Ned went back to help them.

In the early morning light, he came slowly out of the trees, his gun in his hand. One man against thirty-four policemen. They fired and fired at him, but the bullets hit Ned's armour, and Ned laughed.

'Go on – fire! You can't kill me!' he called.

But there was no armour on Ned's legs. One of the policemen saw this, and fired – once, twice . . . The bullets hit Ned's legs, and he fell slowly to the ground.

At once the police were all around him. He was alive, but only just, and they carried him to the railway station.

Soon after this, the last hostages left Glenrowan Inn.

Ned's last fight

Only Dan and Steve were still inside, but the police did not stop firing at the building. Later on that Monday morning a second train arrived in Glenrowan, with more police, photographers, and newspaper men. There were now more than a thousand people in the town. And down south, in Melbourne, hundreds of people waited in the streets for news of the Kelly Gang.

On Monday afternoon Ned's sisters, Maggie and Kate, arrived in Glenrowan. They heard the news about Ned, and then asked for news of Dan.

'Maggie, tell your brother and Steve Hart to put down their guns and come out of the inn,' said a policeman.

'Tell them to stop fighting? Never!' said Maggie.

Maggie and Kate did not see Dan alive again. The police were afraid to go into the inn, but they did not want Dan and Steve to get away in the night. So they set fire to the building.

Old buildings burn fast, and when Maggie and Kate got to the inn, the sky was red with fire.

'Dan! Oh, Dan!' Maggie called out, again and again.

'My poor, poor brother!' Kate cried.

x x x

Glenrowan Inn burnt down to the ground. When the fire was cold, they took out the dead bodies of Dan Kelly, Steve Hart, and Joe Byrne. Ned was alive, but in prison. It was the end of the Kelly Gang.

Glenrowan Inn, burning

Glenrowan Inn, after the fire

6
Ned's last days

JULY, 1880. The police take Ned Kelly to Benalla, then to Melbourne prison. There is a lot of waiting, and talking, and more talking. The police talk, the judges talk, Ned talks – but the ending is always the same.

x x x

At the end of October Ned went before his last judge, Sir Redmond Barry, in Melbourne. For two days Judge Barry listened to the police, listened to Ned, read the police papers, and thought about it. But he didn't think long. There were a lot of dead policemen in Ned Kelly's life, and there was only one answer to that.

Ned Kelly must die. Hang him in the prison. Hang him by the neck until he is dead. A lesson to every outlaw in Australia.

x x x

Ned's mother Ellen was still in Melbourne prison. When they told her the news, she cried – she cried for her dead son Dan, and she cried for her son Ned, alive, but waiting to die. They took her to see Ned on his last day alive. What did mother and son talk about that day?

Ned's sisters and brother worked hard to help him.

'How can they do this?' said Maggie angrily. 'How can

Ned Kelly before the judge, Sir Redmond Barry

they hang poor Ned? What did the police do to *him*? Why don't the judges think about *that*?'

'Shh, Maggie,' said Jim. 'No time for that now. We must get out there and talk to the people in the town.'

And so they did. They went all round Melbourne, to all the hotels, talking to everybody.

'They're going to hang Ned Kelly. What do you think about that?' they asked.

'It's not right,' said one man.

'Why do they want to hang him?' a second man said.

'Because he killed a policeman? No. Because he helps poor people and gives them money, that's why.'

'But what can we do?' asked a third man.

'Put your names on our petition,' was the answer.

There were more than 32,000 names on the Kelly petition, but the petition changed nothing.

So the last visitors came to see Ned on the 10th of November, and he ate his last dinner. Then he sang for half an hour, and went to bed.

Next morning they took Ned across the prison to a room with a rope.

The room with the rope . . .
[A famous drawing from the Australasian Sketcher *newspaper]*

Outside the prison more than 5000 people waited – men and women, rich and poor.

'Where's the Kelly family?' one woman asked.

'Some of them are here, at the hotel,' was the answer. 'But Maggie went back to Beechworth yesterday. She wanted to be with her children. And there's Ned's poor mother – she's in the prison too, waiting for ten o'clock.'

Then the prisoners in Melbourne prison began to make a terrible noise, shouting and crying out and banging on their doors. And in her room Ellen Kelly cried quietly for her oldest son.

In the hotel Jim Kelly sat with his head in his hands.

'Poor Ned, this is the end of all his troubles,' he said.

And at ten o'clock, the prison officers put the rope around Ned Kelly's neck and hanged him.

✗ ✗ ✗

Ned was dead – but in the north-east, life went on. Sixty-eight people got money from the Kelly Gang reward. Schoolteacher Thomas Curnow got £1000.

A new man, Policeman Graham, came to Greta. He was a good policeman, and Ned's friends listened to him. 'Don't make trouble, and then you can buy your farms,' he told them. He went to Eleven Mile Creek and had tea with Ellen Kelly. Everyone talked about that.

Slowly things began to change. The police tried to be more friendly, to help poor people, and not just the rich.

*Ellen Kelly in 1911,
with two of her granddaughters*

Most of the young men stopped stealing and fighting the police. Soon it was quiet in the north-east.

The other Kelly children stayed out of trouble. Jim Kelly was a good son to his mother all her life. Ellen lived to the age of ninety-three, and had many grandchildren. But she never forgot her oldest son Ned.

✕ ✕ ✕

Who was the *real* Ned Kelly? Did he fight for the poor, or just for Ned Kelly? Some people say he was a brave man. Some people say he was a fool. Some people say he was just a killer, just a wild man with a gun.

One thing is sure. More than a hundred years later people are still talking about him. There are books about him, and songs and films and websites. Everybody still remembers Australia's most famous outlaw.

GLOSSARY

armour metal clothes that protect you when you are fighting
belong if something belongs to you, it is yours
brave not afraid to do dangerous things
bullet a small piece of metal that comes out of a gun
burn to be on fire
camp *(n & v)* a place where people live in tents for a short time
crime something bad which is against the law
cut *(v)* to make a hole in something with a knife
editor the most important person in a newspaper office
fall (past tense **fell**) to go down quickly from a high place
farm land and buildings where people grow things to eat and
keep animals for food
fight *(v & n)* to hit, hurt, or try to kill someone
fire *(n)* something burning
fire *(v)* to shoot with a gun
fool a stupid person; not quick at understanding or learning
gang a group of people who do bad things together
hang (past tense **hanged**) to kill somebody by holding them
above the ground by a rope around their neck
hard difficult
hide (past tense **hid**) to go to or be in a place where people
cannot see you or find you
hostage a prisoner that you keep until people do what you want
inn a building where you can buy food and drink
judge the person who decides when somebody must go to prison
jump to move quickly with both feet off the ground
justice when things are fair and right for everybody
land a piece of ground

light *(n)* to see in the dark, you need a light

lock *(v)* to close (a door, box, etc.) with a key

newspaper people buy this every day to read about the things happening in the world (the news)

officer a person with an important job, often in the government

outlaw a person who does bad things and lives outside the law

petition a special letter, from a large group of people, that asks for something

plan *(v & n)* to decide what you are going to do and how to do it

policeman policemen try to stop crime and to catch bad people

print *(v)* to put words onto paper using a machine

prison a building for bad people; they stay there and cannot leave

reward money for helping the police find a bad person

rob to steal money or things from a person or place

rope very thick, strong string

set fire to to start a fire and make something burn

shoot (past tense **shot**) to send a bullet from a gun and kill or hurt somebody

shout to speak or call out very loudly

station a building where trains arrive, or where policemen work

steal (past tense **stole**) to take something which is not yours

stolen *(adj)* taken from another person

strong a strong person can carry heavy things

take care of to make someone happy and comfortable

terrible something terrible makes you very afraid or unhappy

tracks a line of marks that feet or shoes make on the ground

trouble problems and difficulties when you do something wrong

wild dangerous, not controlled

wound *(n)* a hurt place in your body, made by a gun or knife

Before Reading

1 **Read the story introduction on the first page of the book, and the back cover. How much do you know now about the story? Tick one box for each sentence.**

	YES	NO
1 Ned was born into a poor family.	☐	☐
2 Ned's mother killed a policeman.	☐	☐
3 Ned tried to live a quiet life.	☐	☐
4 Ned took other people's horses.	☐	☐
5 Policemen tried to help Ned and his brothers.	☐	☐
6 Ned was a real person.	☐	☐

2 **What is going to happen in the story? Can you guess? Choose endings for these sentences.**

1 Ned Kelly shoots and kills . . .

  a) his brother.   c) another outlaw.

  b) a rich farmer.   d) a policeman.

2 Ned steals from . . .

  a) banks.   c) his friends.

  b) people in towns.   d) women.

3 At the end of the story Ned is . . .

  a) rich.   c) dead.

  b) married.   d) a father.

While Reading

Read page 1, and Chapters 1 and 2. Then complete each sentence with the right name or names.

1 _____ went to prison after he stole a cow.

2 _____ took her family to the northeast.

3 _____ had a terrible fight with Policeman Hall.

4 _____ died before Ned came home from prison.

5 _____ and Ned stole a lot of horses and sold them.

6 _____ liked Ned's sister Kate.

7 _____ fired at the policeman in his house.

8 _____ and _____ joined the Kelly brothers at Bullock Creek.

How do you feel about these people in the story? Put a circle round one answer for each person.

Do you feel sorry for these people?

1 Ellen Kelly   *yes / a little / no*

2 Policeman Hall   *yes / a little / no*

3 Kate   *yes / a little / no*

4 Ned   *yes / a little / no*

5 Dan   *yes / a little / no*

6 Policeman Fitzpatrick   *yes / a little / no*

Read Chapter 3. Are these sentences true (T) or false (F)? Change the false sentences into true ones.

1 The police planned to catch the Kelly Gang and bring them back alive.
2 Ned and Dan found the police camp easily.
3 Ned shot Lonigan when he ran out of the camp.
4 Kennedy laughed when McIntyre said, 'There are men with guns here.'
5 Ned did not want to kill any policemen.
6 There was a reward of land or horses for news of every man in the Kelly Gang.
7 Ned and the gang stayed in the northeast because they wanted to be near to their families.
8 The police often saw the outlaws but they could not catch them.

Read Chapter 4. Then answer these questions.

Why

1 . . . did the police put the Gang's friends in prison?
2 . . . did the Kelly Gang rob a bank?
3 . . . did Ned write a letter to the world?
4 . . . did the police go to Corryong?
5 . . . did Ned go to the newspaper editor's house?
6 . . . did nobody get the reward?
7 . . . didn't the letter go into the newspaper?

Before you read Chapter 5, can you guess what happens? Choose some of these answers.

1 The police shoot Ned.

2 The gang take some hostages.

3 Dan, Joe, and Steve get away.

4 Dan, Joe, and Steve die.

5 The gang kill a lot of policemen.

6 The gang take a lot of money from a bank.

7 A train comes off the railway line and a lot of people die.

8 The gang hide in a school.

Read Chapters 5 and 6. What do you think about Ned Kelly's story? Choose Yes (Y) or No (N) for each of these sentences.

1 Ellen Kelly was a bad mother to her children. Y/N

2 Maggie, Kate, and Jim were wrong to start a petition. Y/N

3 It was right to hang Ned Kelly. Y/N

4 It was right for Thomas Curnow to get a reward. Y/N

5 Ned Kelly was a brave man and a good man. Y/N

6 Edwin Living was wrong to take the letter to the police. Y/N

7 The police were wrong to set fire to the inn. Y/N

8 Ned's friends were right to help him and the gang. Y/N

9 Ned was right to send his friends away from Glenrowan. Y/N

After Reading

1 Perhaps this is what some of the people in the story are thinking at different times. Who are they, where are they, and what are they doing at this point in the story?

1 'They can't do that to the train! That's terrible! But what can I do? Perhaps I can say to him, "Ned, you know me – I'm your friend. Can we take the baby home?" Then I can run down the railway line and stop the train . . .'

2 'Go on, shoot me! I'm going back into the inn, and you can't stop me. Your bullets can't kill me. Ah, aaah! My legs – oh, my legs . . . I can't . . . I'm going to fall . . .'

3 'Where's my horse? I must get back to the station. They're going to pay for this, those Kellys. Ow! Careful now. Can I ride with one hand? Yes, I think so . . .'

4 'My hand gets tired, writing all these pages. But he talks so well – it's important to get every word down. He's talking for all of us, and the world must listen . . .'

5 'I'm never going to see him again, never. The time is nearly here – yes, I can hear the clock now. Oh, my boy, my boy. You were a brave man, and a good son . . .'

2 Here is a new illustration for the story. Find the best place in the story to put the picture, and answer these questions.

The picture goes on page _____.

1 What are the gang making?
2 What are they going to do with it?
3 How is it going to help them?

Now write a caption for the illustration.

Caption: _____

3 Find these words in the word search below, and draw lines through them. The words go from left to right, and from top to bottom.

armour, brave, bullet, fall, fight, fire, gang, hostage, inn, judge, justice, outlaw, petition, plan, reward, rob, rope, shoot, shout, strong, trouble, wild

F	A	L	L	R	H	F	S	T	R	O	N	G
I	R	E	W	E	A	I	H	B	S	P	P	A
G	M	B	R	W	A	R	O	U	V	L	E	E
H	O	S	T	A	G	E	U	L	J	A	T	M
T	U	A	R	R	A	N	T	L	U	N	I	B
R	R	B	O	D	N	U	T	E	S	W	T	R
O	I	J	U	D	G	E	T	T	T	I	I	A
B	W	A	B	S	H	O	O	T	I	L	O	V
O	U	T	L	A	W	S	H	I	C	D	N	E
R	O	P	E	M	O	I	N	N	E	R	M	E

Now write down all the letters that do not have lines through them, beginning with the first line and going across each line to the end. You now have 29 letters, which make a sentence of 11 words.

1 What is the sentence?
2 Who says it, and where?
3 Who is he talking about?

51

4 Here is a letter from Kate Kelly to her brother Jim. Use these words (one for each gap) to complete the letter.

afraid, around, away, baby, care, door, happen, hour, past, prison, soon, station, suddenly, terrible, today, wanted, wrist

DEAR JIM, I have some _____ news. Last night Policeman Fitzgerald came here. He _____ to take Dan to the police _____. When I walked _____ him, he tried to put his arm _____ me. _____ Ned was at the _____, and he shot Fitzgerald in the _____. The policeman ran out of the door and rode _____. Ned and Dan left the house an _____ later. Then _____ ten policemen came and took Ma and _____ Alice away. I'm taking _____ of the children, but I'm _____, Jim. Is Ma going to go to _____? What's going to _____ to Ned and Dan? Please write _____.

Your unhappy sister, Kate

5 **What did you think about the people in this story? Choose some names, and complete some of these sentences.**

Ned / Ellen Kelly / Aaron Sherritt / Kennedy / McIntyre / Thomas Curnow

1 I liked _____ because _____.
2 I didn't like _____ because _____.
3 I felt sorry for _____ when _____.
4 _____ was right to _____.
5 _____ was wrong to _____

ABOUT THE AUTHOR
AND THE STORY

Christine Lindop was born in New Zealand and taught English in France and Spain before settling in Great Britain. She has written or co-written more than twenty books, including several Bookworms titles – *Goldfish* (Stage 3), *Sally's Phone* (Starters), and *Australia and New Zealand* (Factfiles). She has also written for the Oxford Dominoes series, and has worked on many Oxford reader series, including Bookworms, Dominoes, Classic Tales, Factfiles, Hotshot Puzzles, and Storylines.

Christine Lindop has been fascinated by Ned Kelly since she saw some of the famous Ned Kelly paintings by Sidney Nolan in the 1970s. 'Even today, more than a hundred years after his death, Australians can't stop talking about him,' she says. 'Everywhere you look, you find Ned Kelly.'

There are at least ten films about Ned Kelly's life. *The Story of the Kelly Gang*, made in 1906, was the first long film ever made. In three later films Ned was played by Godfrey Cass, who was the son of the prison governor in Melbourne. Godfrey, aged fourteen at the time, met Ned in prison on the day before he died.

You can find Ned Kelly on stamps, on T-shirts, and on bottles. There are Ned Kelly songs, Ned comics, and hundreds of books about him. If you go to Australia, you can stay in a Ned Kelly hotel and have your photograph taken in Ned Kelly armour – and then drink your coffee from a little Ned Kelly helmet. Even Homer Simpson has appeared in Ned Kelly armour! Hero or villain, Ned Kelly still gets people as excited today as he did in the 1870s.

OXFORD BOOKWORMS LIBRARY

Classics • Crime & Mystery • Factfiles • Fantasy & Horror
Human Interest • Playscripts • Thriller & Adventure
True Stories • World Stories

The OXFORD BOOKWORMS LIBRARY provides enjoyable reading in English, with a wide range of classic and modern fiction, non-fiction, and plays. It includes original and adapted texts in seven carefully graded language stages, which take learners from beginner to advanced level. An overview is given on the next pages.

All Stage 1 titles are available as audio recordings, as well as over eighty other titles from Starter to Stage 6. All Starters and many titles at Stages 1 to 4 are specially recommended for younger learners. Every Bookworm is illustrated, and Starters and Factfiles have full-colour illustrations.

The OXFORD BOOKWORMS LIBRARY also offers extensive support. Each book contains an introduction to the story, notes about the author, a glossary, and activities. Additional resources include tests and worksheets, and answers for these and for the activities in the books. There is advice on running a class library, using audio recordings, and the many ways of using Oxford Bookworms in reading programmes. Resource materials are available on the website <www.oup.com/bookworms>.

The *Oxford Bookworms Collection* is a series for advanced learners. It consists of volumes of short stories by well-known authors, both classic and modern. Texts are not abridged or adapted in any way, but carefully selected to be accessible to the advanced student.

———

You can find details and a full list of titles in the *Oxford Bookworms Library Catalogue* and *Oxford English Language Teaching Catalogues*, and on the website <www.oup.com/bookworms>.

THE OXFORD BOOKWORMS LIBRARY
GRADING AND SAMPLE EXTRACTS

STARTER • 250 HEADWORDS

present simple – present continuous – imperative –
can/cannot, must – going to (future) – simple gerunds ...

Her phone is ringing – but where is it?

Sally gets out of bed and looks in her bag. No phone. She looks under the bed. No phone. Then she looks behind the door. There is her phone. Sally picks up her phone and answers it. *Sally's Phone*

STAGE 1 • 400 HEADWORDS

... past simple – coordination with *and*, *but*, *or* –
subordination with *before*, *after*, *when*, *because*, *so* ...

I knew him in Persia. He was a famous builder and I worked with him there. For a time I was his friend, but not for long. When he came to Paris, I came after him – I wanted to watch him. He was a very clever, very dangerous man. *The Phantom of the Opera*

STAGE 2 • 700 HEADWORDS

... present perfect – *will* (future) – *(don't) have to, must not, could* –
comparison of adjectives – simple *if* clauses – past continuous
tag questions – *ask/tell* + infinitive ...

While I was writing these words in my diary, I decided what to do. I must try to escape. I shall try to get down the wall outside. The window is high above the ground, but I have to try. I shall take some of the gold with me – if I escape, perhaps it will be helpful later. *Dracula*

... should, may – present perfect continuous – *used to* – past perfect –
causative – relative clauses – indirect statements ...

Of course, it was most important that no one should see
Colin, Mary, or Dickon entering the secret garden. So Colin
gave orders to the gardeners that they must all keep away
from that part of the garden in future. ***The Secret Garden***

... past perfect continuous – passive (simple forms) –
would conditional clauses – indirect questions –
relatives with *where/when* – gerunds after prepositions/phrases ...

I was glad. Now Hyde could not show his face to the world
again. If he did, every honest man in London would be proud
to report him to the police. ***Dr Jekyll and Mr Hyde***

... future continuous – future perfect –
passive (modals, continuous forms) –
would have conditional clauses – modals + perfect infinitive ...

If he had spoken Estella's name, I would have hit him. I was so
angry with him, and so depressed about my future, that I could
not eat the breakfast. Instead I went straight to the old house.
Great Expectations

... passive (infinitives, gerunds) – advanced modal meanings –
clauses of concession, condition

When I stepped up to the piano, I was confident. It was as if I
knew that the prodigy side of me really did exist. And when I
started to play, I was so caught up in how lovely I looked that
I didn't worry how I would sound. ***The Joy Luck Club***